D0506054

NEV WILSHIRE

HAPPY
PEOPLE
SELL

BOOKS

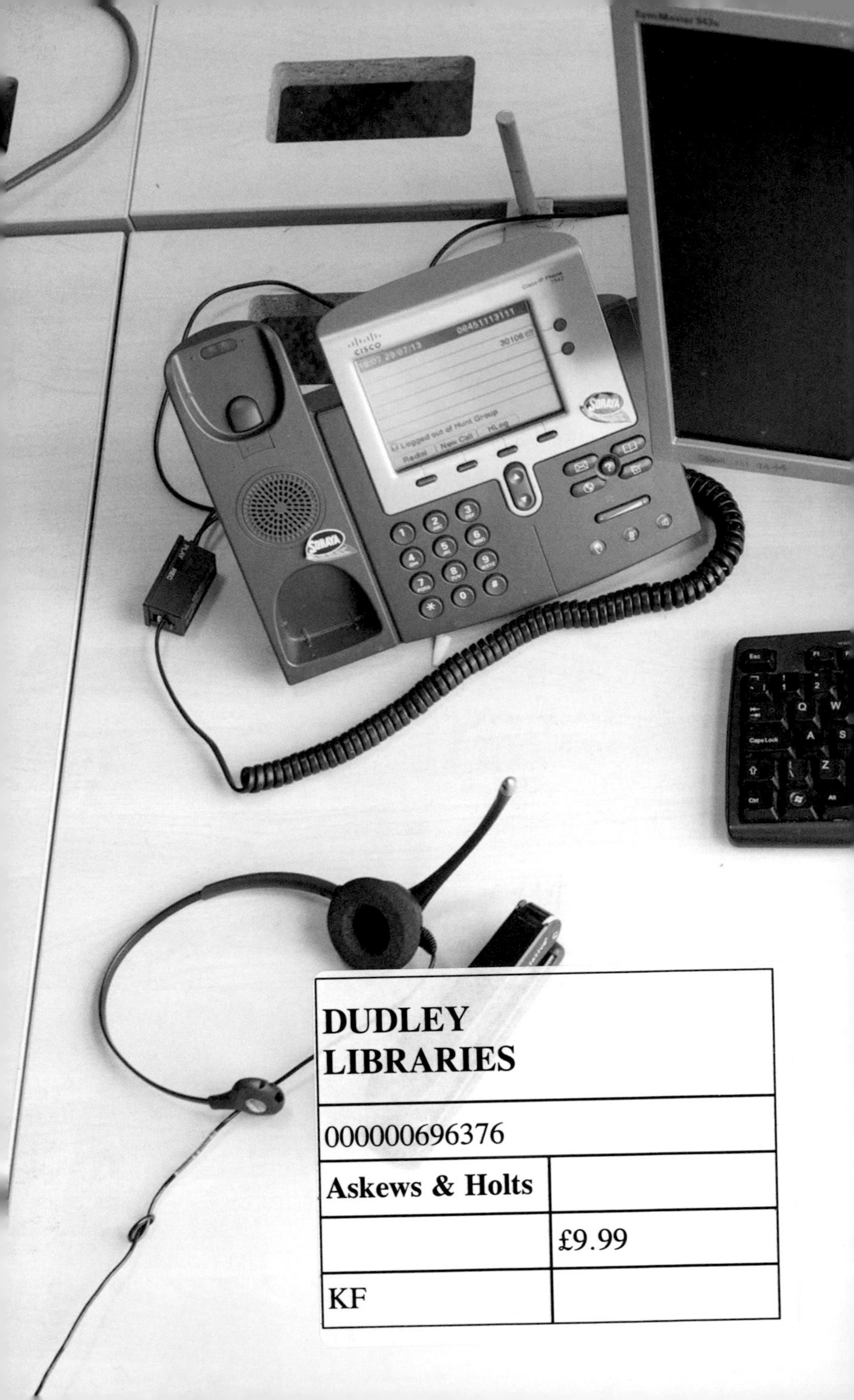
CISCO
Logged out of Hunt Group
Redial
New Call
SORAYA

NEV WILSHIRE

HAPPY PEOPLE
SELL

BOOKS

CONTENTS

Introduction Happy people sell 7

Chapter 1 Life lessons 11

Chapter 2 Starting a business 21

Chapter 3 Recruitment 29

Chapter 4 Training 39

Chapter 5 Creating team spirit 47

Chapter 6 The office environment 61

Chapter 7 Be a leader 69

Chapter 8 Dare to be different 77

Chapter 9 Office relationships 85

Chapter 10 Maintaining discipline 93

Chapter 11 The perfect telesale 105

Chapter 12 Tough times 121

Chapter 13 Communications 127

Chapter 14 Work–life balance 133

Chapter 15 Follow your dreams 139

'Firstly, thanks for buying my book. If you haven't bought it and are just flicking through it in a book shop, then stop being so tight and buy it!'

INTRODUCTION

I'm Nev, I'm going to sort out your business problems... or add to them!

You may be thinking why would anyone want to follow my guidance when I'm a total arsehole? Well, reason no. 1: I started my company with nothing and now we've achieved a £50 million turnover. Reason no. 2: I employ over 600 staff who love being employed by me so much that this year we came second on the *Sunday Times* list of The Best Companies To Work For in the UK. Which proves there must be some method in my madness!

I never expected to be on the telly, but last year the BBC came calling and now out of the blue I'm a flippin' TV personality. How did that happen? So far it has been a terrific roller-coaster ride for all of us at the call centre and I'm honoured that people are now looking to me for inspiration.

In this book I'll be covering my tips and techniques for effective staff management including arm-wrestling, matchmaking and compulsory singing! I've also written about my inspirational leadership techniques and the secrets of the 'sales-with-a-smile' approach I've used to build my company.

Happiness in the workplace won't necessarily mean your business will achieve better results – but it gives you a much better chance and it will definitely be a far nicer place to work. If you're happy, the opposite sex are attracted to you. Fact. People don't want to be around miserable people. Fact. Being happy and upbeat is going to improve your business environment. Fact. Happy people sell. FACT.

It doesn't cost anything to be enthusiastic and cheerful and if this book leads to just one more board meeting starting with a rendition of 'Mr Brightside', then my work here is done...

Nev Wilshire

Founder and CEO of the Save Britain Money group

Now GET OUT!

'Fruit grows in the valleys not on the mountain tops.'

Life lessons

The truth is when you are having a mountain-top experience and you're right up there with your flash car and all the trappings of success, you're not always learning. It can feel like you're on a high where no-one can touch you, but it's often a barren place. I've had highs and I've had lows but it was when I was down that I learnt life's biggest lessons and it's those experiences combined that have made me the successful character I am today.

When I was a kid we had sod all. My dad was a student and Mum was a housewife. Money was scarce but there was plenty of love. They were living on a caravan site in the village of Pennard, just outside

Swansea, which was the cheapest place they could find to call home, when I came along (the middle child of three brothers). Dad used to sweat his nuts off getting scholarships to make ends meet. In later years Mum cut our hair herself and our nan knitted us jumpers to keep us warm. I remember my mates stopping at the sweet shop on the way to school, but I couldn't. We didn't have any money for luxuries like sweets and the thought of buying any wouldn't have even entered my head. As my brother Keith and I later reflected kids of today wouldn't have coped but we couldn't have been happier. I wouldn't have swapped it for anything.

'I've had highs and I've had lows but it was when I was down that I learnt life's biggest lessons.'

I was a lazy slob at school because I always preferred to entertain the class rather than do any work – once the joker always the joker! I may not have been the most academic of pupils but I loved sport and being at school taught me the difference between right and wrong. When I finished my O-levels I started knocking on doors to find a part-time job in order to fund my sixth-form social life. I struck gold when I was taken on to work Saturdays and school holidays under Mr Bryn Morgan, a lovely man in his 60s, in the suit department at the Thomas Thomas's Warehouse in Swansea. He taught me a lot – how to keep everything tidy, that first impressions make a big difference and how to engage with customers. It was my first sales job and I took to it like a duck to water. I later worked in the electrical department where I learnt to tell the truth rather than blagging your way through and looking an arsehole!

Of course, you don't always get to work for a boss like that. In my time I've seen some absolute arseholes – a real shock to the system after the camaraderie of somewhere like Thomas Thomas's. Why you'd want to spend your days creating a demoralising environment, insulting the customers, insulting the staff or generally upsetting everyone for a few hours a day before pissing off again is beyond me. I've always had a natural enthusiasm for work, but – then and now – I'd rather sweep the streets than work for someone like that.

I got another education in sales – and the world of central heating – when I was taken on at a firm called

'I was so angry that if I'd had a gun, I don't know what I would have done.'

Heateck, where I soon became one of their youngest but biggest selling reps. By 24 I was married with two children and felt confident I had the know-how to start my own business. In 1984 I set up Central Heating Services, a plumber's merchant, and we got off to a flying start making £100,000 profit in the first year. I lived a millionaire's lifestyle but then the recession hit. No-one had seen it coming and even though I was battling to turn things around, the bank put the company into receivership because of our increasing debts. It was a tough time all around. People I expected to be my friends shat on me, I lost my home and it contributed to my divorce. I was on my arse, basically. I couldn't even get dole and I was living off selling my possessions at car boot sales. There were times I was hungry and I even slept rough for a couple of nights. Eventually I had to move in with my parents which, let's face it, no-one wants to do as a grown adult.

The big lesson I learnt at that time is not to trust anyone else to look after your finances (always keep an eye on the books) and never put your faith in a bank. There was no reason for Central Heating Services to go bust, but it felt like the bank kept moving the goalposts. We discovered that they'd overcharged us by £70,000, and when I pointed this out to the bank manager, he just called the receivers in before it was properly investigated. I was so angry that if I'd had a gun, I don't know what I would have done. Little bastard – putting me through all that and hiding behind bank policy!

It was thanks to Walt Disney (it's a long story, see Chapter 12!) that I pulled myself out of the doldrums and soon I was back on the road as an energy surveyor, helping people on low incomes improve their homes with new central heating systems funded by the Welsh Assembly and the power companies. There were all these grants being given out but no-one knew about them and I began to realise there was a huge business opportunity here.

Tapping into that market I felt ready to set up on my own again and Nationwide Energy Services was born in 2005. Initially we employed just 12 people, but it grew and grew – now we have over 600 employees based in our offices in Swansea and up to 500 support staff working out in the field. I'd caught a break, I'd been given a second chance and I was grabbing it with both hands.

That business is now part of my group of companies called Save Britain Money, which does what it says on the tin and sets out to save people cash on their bills. We started on one floor of our current premises, four years later we bought the bloody building! It's phenomenal what we've all achieved, but one of the biggest lessons I've learnt along the way as a businessman, through all the ups and downs, is that the only person you can truly rely on is yourself. And if you're unreliable, what chance have you got?

'We started on one floor of our current premises, four years later we bought the bloody building!'

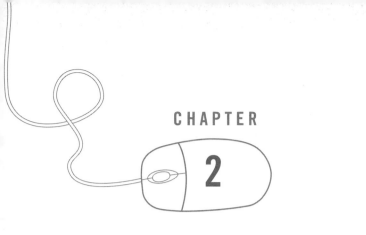

CHAPTER

2

'Many wish, some plan, few do.'

Starting a business

Identifying the opportunity

Don't hunt high and low for a random business idea,
a much better course is to start a business based
on a need you have that isn't being met by existing
suppliers. Look at Walt Disney. Disneyland came from
his frustration at the lack of suitable options when
he wanted to take his grandchildren out for the day
in California, so he came up with an idea for a place
where families could have fun together.

Look at Sir Richard Branson. Why did he start Virgin
Atlantic? Because he was flying back from America

on British Airways and was bored shitless – the seat wasn't very comfy and there wasn't any entertainment. He thought, 'Surely I can do better than this?' So off he went and did it better. They both used their own life experiences. Keep an eye out for good ideas that are poorly executed and then work out how you can do them differently, cheaper or better than anybody else.

There's a big element of luck too. Sometimes an opportunity lands in your lap, but it's up to you to have the brains or the canniness to do something with it. Sometimes you don't see the opportunity even if it's right there under your nose. Stick to what you know and don't remortgage your house on an idea unless you have identified potential customers, tested and researched it. If there isn't a market for it – jog on! Don't get emotionally attached to a dead-end scheme.

'Keep an eye out for good ideas that are poorly executed and work out how you can do them better.'

Start small

Every business I've owned has started small and Sir Richard started Virgin Atlantic with just one plane. It's the best way to launch a new venture unless you've got more money than sense. You can have grand ideas, but don't get too ambitious before you've even started. Get the ball into play and start chasing it as soon as you can, because until you do you're not going to make any money.

The name game

Bosses are often tempted to name companies after themselves – don't! For most customers your name will be meaningless in relation to the product. The company name also needs to sound right when it's said aloud, you really don't want to be repeating yourself every time you pick up the flippin' phone. When in doubt the best solution is to say what it does. E.g.: My company Save Britain Money does what it says on the tin and is also a name that can work across countless products and services as the company grows.

Be organised

Preparation is key. Proper planning prevents piss-poor performance. With any new venture you're always organising the way forward and tweaking to make sure everything falls into place. Looking at the bigger picture you need to start mapping out where you're going to take the business longterm.

'Proper planning prevents piss poor performance.'

The Lord blesses the work of your hand – so make sure you work!

Get out there and slog. Nothing comes to you if you're sitting on your arse all day... unless you're a computer programmer! I'm a natural born grafter and when you're slogging for yourself there's even more incentive to work hard. I believe that work ethic is either in you or it isn't and if you've always been a lazy bastard you're not going to suddenly work harder just because you're working for yourself.

Love your business

Years ago I was chatting to a Swedish business associate and he said to me, 'You know Nev, the problem with you English... [Because we all are English to them]...is you're in business for the wrong reasons.' I said, 'What do you mean, Gunther?' He explained, 'In England you're in business for your four acres, your double garage and your horse. Over here we LOVE our businesses. We make Volvo, we make Saab. They are the best, we build the best, we ARE the best.' And he was right.

The Germans have the same mindset with their Porsche and Mercedes cars, but in the UK we aren't passionate or patriotic about our companies in the same way. What I took away from that conversation is that you've got to LOVE your business, whether you're selling plastic bags, sausage skins or cardboard boxes. If you're setting up a new enterprise you've got to choose an industry that you're genuinely interested in. You must have a passion for your product. If your heart isn't in it you're in the wrong line of work and your business is unlikely to flourish.

CHAPTER

3

'I favour those with a glide in their stride.'

Recruitment

The late, great football manager Brian Clough once said 'surround yourself with good people and the rest is easy' and I couldn't agree more. Strategically place talented people around you and make sure they have a glide in their stride. What I mean by that is when you see Chickenhead strutting through the office, even though he can be a complete dick at times, he's got the swagger, he's got that glide in his stride. Truth be told he thinks he's the dog's bollocks. But what that swagger, bravado and self-belief add up to is confidence. And I want to employ confident people.

You can learn a lot about a prospective employee by the way they put one foot in front of the other. If they amble along the street with their head down without any sense of intent they aren't right for the job. But if they're striding with a sense of purpose and their head held high... that's the kind of person I want on my team. I'm not suggesting you follow all your potential employees down the street (that's stalking isn't it?) but it is important to consider an applicant's demeanour when recruiting.

To work for me you've got to be resilient, upbeat and – wait for it, I think you know what's coming next – HAPPY. If you're too cool for school or have a face like a smacked arse then you just won't fit in. I'm a naturally happy person, that's just me. I'm not saying my employees have to be upbeat and grinning like lunatics all the time. But you do need to be enthusiastic, polite and able to get over to the customer that there are benefits for them in the product you are selling. For that reason I always hire mindset and attitude over skills and qualifications. Ultimately your staff are your most prized asset so I strive to treat my employees and my customers with equal care and commitment.

'I hire mindset and attitude over skills and experience.'

The walk of shame

Marching prospective staff members up and down the call centre shouting 'Good-looking Welsh girl coming through, can she have a job?' may not be politically correct, but it's something I do regularly. It isn't about trying to humiliate that person, it's about how they respond to the banter. If they're laughing and enjoying it they have passed the first test because it shows they have the confidence. If they're scared shitless or look like they want to cry it's unlikely they are going to fit in. The HR department despairs of me in situations like this – they're just trying to do their jobs and cover my arse, but I like to mix things up and give them something to worry about.

'The HR department despairs of me in situations like this but I like to give them something to worry about.'

On the radio

We often work with local radio to do a recruitment drive. I'll go on air and say, 'If you need a job we're looking to interview people today, so get off your arse, get in your car, scrounge a lift, because we are interviewing for jobs RIGHT NOW.' I found when we took on people sent to us by the job centre they'd just sit there all day yawning, they didn't want to be there. But by doing a radio recruitment drive you've already wheedled out the lazy ones. It creates an excitement and a buzz around the business and anyone who has bothered to immediately get off their backside and come in must have some desire and an enthusiasm for work.

Stand and deliver

Someone who'd been recommended to me came in for an interview. She was a law graduate and was clearly capable and intelligent, but was incredibly timid and self-conscious. I realised I needed to draw her out of herself to see if she could survive in this madhouse. So I stood on my desk. I said, 'I'm going to interview you from up here now.' She looked startled and by now the whole call centre was watching us through the glass thinking, 'What's Nev doing this time?' Then I told her if she didn't relax I was going to shout at her to GET OUT in front of everyone. 'You're not going to shout at me...' she says, bottom lip trembling. 'Oh yes I am. Unless you relax and answer my questions properly. Are you going to do that?' Then she started laughing. So I got down, she gave a great interview and she's still working for me now. People think I'm bonkers for standing on my desk like that but it breaks the ice and gets over the fact that we aren't a scary company. Interviewees don't have to be in awe of the boss. You just have to be yourself and you'll get the job.

'People think I'm bonkers for standing on my desk'.

To: nevtheboss@savebritainmoney.co.uk
From: becca_HR@savebritainmoney.co.uk

Subject: **Interview technique**

Nev

Remember, it is strictly against company policy to conduct interviews from *on top* of office furniture. Please DO NOT make any reference to this in your book, or we'll get in trouble with health and safety.

Becca

'Happy people sing.'

Training

It isn't fair to the customer if I put someone on the phone who hasn't got a clue what they're talking about. If you don't know the product you can't sell it, and if the customer knows more than you do, you're definitely fighting a losing battle. The lesson is your workforce are only as good as the training they receive.

New recruits need to be enthused about the company they're joining and that's why I believe in the power of song. Singing makes you happy. Fact. So I thought, 'These people are coming into a big company for the first time and it's going to be daunting. Let's get some barriers down. We're all in the same boat, we're going to have a sing-song and enjoy the happiness that comes when you're singing together. It usually takes three songs for people to start to relax and get rid of their inhibitions.'

From an employee's very first day with the company I want to create a mindset of camaraderie and enthusiasm. Most of them will sing, some of them will pretend, but if you're up yourself and refuse to join in you may as well bugger off right now rather than waste my time. Shit or bust, what's it going to be?

The first number we ever did in training was Guns N' Roses 'Sweet Child o' Mine', not a song you can mumble. I led the way belting it out telling them, 'We're all going to be Slash now... get out your air guitars people!' Half of them thought I was round the twist. Nowadays I start with 'Mr Brightside' by The Killers which I think is my all-time favourite song. It never fails to put a smile on my face.

The singing is motivational: it lifts your spirits and gets you enthused about the employment opportunity. It indicates this is going to be a fun place to work and that they are going to enjoy being here. It's only their first day yet they are already feeling positive about the company. We always ask newbies to fill out a feedback-form and one of the questions is 'What was the best part of training?'. Guess what? Nearly everyone says 'Singing with Nev'. So we must be doing something right.

This job can be hard and singing is a good way to let go of your inhibitions. You know you're going to get on the phone and sooner or later you'll be on the receiving end of abuse and name-calling. So you need to get confident, get a thick skin, be able to shrug off any bad experiences and switch on that smile for the next dial.

'I believe in the power of song.'

Sing when you're winning

If you want to maintain a happy persona, whatever you do don't sing loser songs. They are the enemy! Stop playing them in your car, burn the CDs, erase them from your mind. Everyone loves a winner, so become one...

Winner songs

Mr Brightside – The Killers
(I'm Gonna Be) 500 Miles – The Proclaimers
Sex On Fire – Kings Of Leon
Tonight's The Night – Black Eyed Peas

Loser songs

Bye Bye Love – The Everly Brothers
Anything by The Smiths
All By Myself – Celine Dion

The Wilshire Fling

Why do I hurl things at people during training?
Because I'm giving up my time to come and speak to
you so you'd better stop yawning and start listening.
You're not at school anymore. You think I reckon I'm
better than you? I'm not. But I've learnt a hell of a lot
more through experience than you have, mate. And if
you think you know more than me, there's the door,
off you go, bugger off.

If someone's yawning it means they don't want to
be there, which means they don't give a monkey's
about the job and if you don't want the job then
thanks very much you can piss off now. It could be a
board rubber, it could be a pen, it could be a sausage
roll. Whatever comes to hand. I threw a spoon once
which hit a glass and it exploded everywhere. That
was a bit of a bastard.

Before I come into a session the trainees are warned
not to yawn when Nev's speaking or
he'll lob something at your heads.
But they still do it. So when all of
a sudden a meat pasty hits them
in the gob they've only got
themselves to blame.

'When a pasty hits them
in the gob they've only got
themselves to blame.'

This guy just came in for a meeting – never met him before in my life! But I beat him too.

Show them who's boss...

● You have to make it clear to recruits that you are not a pushover. It's all about gaining their respect, so if anyone gets cocky I arm-wrestle them. I remember once there were these two beefed-up lads sitting there like they knew it all, giving it the big 'I am'. I said to one of them, 'You've got big arms haven't you?' 'Yeah, I'm a cage fighter,' he says. 'Okay. Do you want to arm-wrestle me for a pound? He laughed and said make it twenty and slapped down a note! And I stuck a £20 note down on the table. So he's looking at me, a fat, bald, 50-something thinking there's one born every minute, but of course I beat him. Respect earned!

I haven't lost a call centre arm-wrestle in four years. Of course this approach doesn't work so well with women who have the ability to turn on the waterworks as required, rendering me useless. I've tried everything but have now accepted that they are just a different species.

'A chain is only as strong as its weakest link.'

Creating team spirit

The first time people come into our building I'm sure they think we're nuts. It may seem like a holiday camp but there's a method in my madness as we have been voted second best place to work in the UK on the *Sunday Times* list.

I truly believe our success is down to the call centre's unique atmosphere. That energy you get from the sales floor, that buzz you feel as soon as you walk in, a lot of companies wish they could bottle it and transfer it into their own workplaces.

First of all it's incredibly important for your staff to think they've got a good job. Okay, working in a call centre isn't the best job in the world. In many ways it's a shit job. You're on the phones bothering people for business and you get called all the names under the sun. So it's not the best job ever, I think we're all agreed on that. But around here in Swansea the better jobs don't exist for these young people and a call centre is likely to be their first rung on the employment ladder. So how do you make the best of it? How do you make people believe that this is a really good place to work? Well, first of all you've got to try and make it a HAPPY place to work. If we didn't have fun people wouldn't stay so long and we'd constantly be looking for new staff.

I have worked in horrible places where you weren't appreciated and where the boss bullied his staff. I've seen first-hand how working in a negative environment can affect your mindset and your work-rate. It's a fact of life – happy people sell, miserable bastards don't.

So I generate team spirit by continually motivating my employees as well as finding reasons to celebrate together. We organise battles of the shifts, parties, outings and we're constantly coming up with new ideas to keep morale sky-high. Let's have a fat bastards club (I'll be signing up for that one), let's dress up as cartoon-characters, let's have a 'Super Duper Day' (we like coming up with stupid names) where you can earn beers to drink after the shift. The sillier the better.

Generally your staff will perform in the way others expect them to perform. So if you treat them as

capable, productive people who can have fun and work at the same time, then that's how they will behave. But if you grind them down and treat them as mediocre, then that's the behaviour you'll get back. A good boss should always expect the best from their staff and treat them accordingly – but that doesn't mean you can't crack an egg over their heads every now and again!

'It's a fact of life – happy people sell, miserable bastards don't.'

Battle of the shifts

In the call centre it's all about motivating the 'what's in it for me' section of society. There isn't a great deal of job satisfaction here, but every time you make a sale that is satisfying. When Twe and Palmer's shifts went against each other their sales went up 20 per cent that month. They'd both put their teams through hell to do it so we decided to bring them down a peg or two. Someone suggested we make them play Russian roulette with eggs, another suggestion was a baked bean eating contest. I said we should do both. It ended up being one of the funniest things I have ever seen and there were benefits all round: the battle of the shifts had been tremendous for productivity and the teams had enjoyed stepping up to the challenge. Then seeing their managers literally with egg on their faces was the icing on the cake (not that there was any cake, but you know what I mean). Everyone was happy, everyone was buzzing and happy buzzy people can only be good for sales.

TEAM
TWE

"YOUR SHIFT NEEDS "

savebritainmoney

The fun factory

A shift in the call centre can be a slog.
Here's how to liven it up...

- We've got a fantastic 'grab a grand
  machine' and the top seller of the
  week gets to go in it. Okay it isn't
  real money (what kind of fool do
  you think I am?), but the final swag
  can be exchanged for some cash.

- Playing games lightens the mood.
  Employees are kept entertained
  which means the day goes faster for
  them. Energy levels stay high which
  means sales are likely to rise too.

- I've been giving out free sweets ever since I've
  had the call centre – you can't beat a sugar rush to
  increase productivity. Keep the sweets flowing, keep
  the beat going. Fill the staff with E numbers and
  they're buzzing away on those phones.

- Prizes = productivity. We've given out a free telly,
  a holiday and even a car before, meaning there are
  plenty of incentives to sell, sell, sell. Competing to be
  the top seller on your team is another motivator.

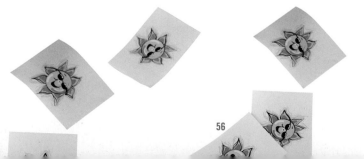

Office parties

We organise a get-together every three months whether it's a piss-up down the pub or a piss-up in a brewery. Parties boost morale and it's a chance to let your hair down whether you're the boss or on the phones. Our Christmas dos are legendary. Last year the house-band The Dialists went down a storm, then Rui (a team leader and a part-time DJ) premiered his dance track called Shit Sandwich which nearly took the roof off. There's so much talent in the call centre and it's great they have an outlet at the parties and that everyone embraces that. We have more fun singing along to The Dialists than if we had Robbie Williams himself there!

Sometimes things go too far. One year our Christmas party got shut down early by the police. The less said about that the better, and yes, I did learn a few lessons about how to organise a party that night. I had to give a full-on headmaster-style bollocking the next day, but shit happens at parties and I've had to shout the odds at people for misbehaving many a time.

'One year our Christmas party got shut down early by the police.'

'Quality environment promotes quality attitude.'

The office environment

I look after my staff in the same way I look after my customers and I want them all to have the best possible experience in their dealings with our company. So a quality working environment promotes a quality working attitude; you can't create that kind of mindset working out of a shit-hole. You should treat people as you want to be treated yourself and the bottom line is I want a nice environment to work in. It's a beautiful building and has to be one of the best office blocks in Swansea. We could make a lot more money if we had much cheaper premises, but I wouldn't want to work in a shit-hole week in week out.

CASE STUDY

Shitting in a bin

You attempt to instil the benefits of respecting the office environment to your staff... and then someone goes and shits in a bin. Why would they shit in a bin in the Ladies' and not the lav? I still can't get my head around it. I said at the time we don't have a company policy on shitting in a bin, it's something we'll have to rectum-fy. We never got to the bottom (no pun intended) of whodunnit, but it speaks volumes about that person's attitude. What you'll find is that the phantom bin-shitter had a bad attitude to sales and a bad attitude to the job. They shit in the bin, their attitude stinks, their bin-shitting stinks, everything about them stinks. If you'd asked them to go and make you a cup of coffee they'd probably gob in it. So, lo and behold, when we got rid of the lowest-achieving sellers, the shitting in the bin problem went with them.

To: nevtheboss@savebritainmoney.co.uk
From: becca_HR@savebritainmoney.co.uk

Subject: **Faeces in the waste receptacle**

Nev

Do we really need to mention this here? Better forgotten? You could talk about the lovely new handwash in the Ladies' instead. Lavender & Lime I think, smells so yummy it almost makes me want to eat my fingers!

Becca

Off her trolley

The kitchen used to get into a right state and I'd be the sap clearing up after them! Everyone goes home and I'm the one loading the bloody dishwasher at 7pm at night? That's not right. Basically they're slobs. It's just like kids never cleaning their bedrooms. So we decided to create a tea-lady position, someone who'd be responsible for serving hot drinks from the trolley, the cleaning and the dishwasher. This would also mean the sales

team wouldn't be out of their seats making a drink every time they wanted to have a skive.

Hayley's sales were down so when she asked if she could be the tea-lady I gave her the job – and she was over the moon. Within two weeks I got a phone call from Twe saying Hayley had crashed the tea trolley. How I do not know. You don't need a licence to drive a tea trolley but somehow Hayley had managed to crash it. So I went down to have a look and found tea and coffee all over the bloody floor, the urns on their sides and everybody else killing themselves laughing. Then she gets the tea and coffee mixed up and puts tea in the coffee and coffee in the tea, because she'd forgotten which one's in which urn. So for the rest of that day we were all drinking bloody T-coffee! She may be nuts, she may be crap at her job, but everybody starts smiling when Hayley's around because she's such a happy, caring person. She's got a big heart and if I can instil that sense of care into everyone that works for me then my work here is done.

Venn diagram illustrating take-up of Hayley's 'T-coffee' amongst employees

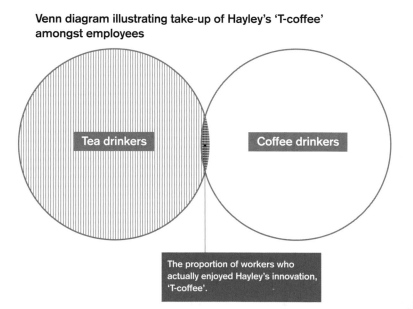

Tea drinkers

Coffee drinkers

The proportion of workers who actually enjoyed Hayley's innovation, 'T-coffee'.

'She may be nuts, but everybody starts smiling when Hayley's around because she's such a happy, caring person.'

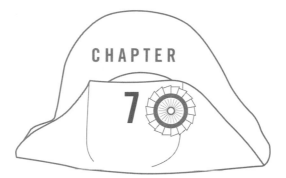

CHAPTER

7

'Big enough to lead, small enough to care.'

Be a leader

To lead is to serve. You serve the people under you, you don't dictate over them. You need to look after your employees and make sure they are equipped to do a good job. If those under you are happy in their work and feel they have a good job, they'll be with you for the long haul. Saying that, though, if people do want to take the piss, out comes Nev the dictator.

Like Napoleon I lead from the front; I don't lead from behind my desk (I'm not sure if Napoleon had a desk, but you get my drift). I'm out there doing what needs to be done because I want the best for my team. Napoleon's people would've laid down their lives for him and they loved him. I'm not sure anyone in the call centre would want to die for me, but some of them do hold me in high regard.

Similarly Napoleon had a passion and a love for his country, while I have a passion and love for the call centre. Anyone working alongside me would tell you that. And like Napoleon I am a benevolent dictator; there's work to be done, we've got to fight the fight, but you have to care about your people along the way. Did it surprise me that Hayley crashed her tea trolley? No. But does she love her work? Yes. The people on the phones, if someone's really trying hard to make something of themselves I'll help them as much as I can. But if someone takes the piss I'll come down on them like a tonne of bricks. A benevolent dictator looks after those below him and while he likes to have a laugh, his people recognise there is a

steeliness there and they know not to cross the line or he will clout them.

Another leader I have a huge respect for is Sir Alex Ferguson – just look at the management skills and the strength of character of that man. The players that came up through his ranks loved him, they idolised him. There are many similarities between managing a football team and running a business. You see, like me throwing a little sausage roll or a pen at somebody, he's been known to throw a dressing-room item or two in his time! Just like on the pitch, in business different participants need to be motivated in different ways. Some need encouragement and an arm around the shoulder, 'Come on now, you're better than that. You're

one of the best
players in the league, get
out there and show them
what you can do.' Others just
need a bollocking, 'You're a fat
lazy bastard, you didn't train
this week and it's showing. Get
out there and perform or I'm
having your nuts for breakfast!'

'Get out there and perform
or I'm having your nuts
for breakfast!'

How to become an inspiring leader

Nurture your staff

Inspiring bosses care about about their employees and nurture them. As Bill Gates once said, 'The fortunate few have an obligation to help those who are less fortunate.'

Command respect

If any of the call-centre kids think they know it all I say, 'I've been where you are. I can do your job, it's a piece of piss. You cannot do what I do… Well, not yet anyway.' You might not like me but you'll show me some bloody respect if you're going to work for me!

Declare the vision

Leaders have ambition and direction. You must clearly impart the strategy to all levels, from sales, support and management, right up to the directors. You must clearly impart the strategy to the management team who will then organise the troops into delivering it.

Make tough calls

I don't think we've had a leader with the courage of their convictions in this country since Margaret Thatcher. As a leader you need the nerve to make big decisions. Because if it all goes tits up it's not your employees' heads on the block, it's yours.

Energise your team

Inspiring leaders boost morale. Staff members should come away from any interaction you have with them thinking, 'Blimey, I really like working for Nev!' You must be able to enthuse fresh-faced new starters and jaded old-timers alike. I utilise the power of song.

'You might not like me but you'll show me some respect if you're going to work for me!'

CHAPTER

8

'To be original is to be yourself.'

Dare to be different

When it comes to selecting a management style don't feel you have to follow the herd. I'm not suggesting your approach has to be the same as mine – i.e. arm-wrestling your employees and riding a horse through the car park – but you need to find a distinctive take on it that suits your personality.

Look at Sir Richard Branson, he has the strength of personality to lead in his own individual way. Never mind how many rungs down the ladder they may be, Sir Richard's enthusiasm filters through to his staff and as a customer you know you'll get a certain level of service from Virgin, whether it's phones or flights.

And that attitude comes from their leader. You get the feeling with Sir Richard it isn't just about the money – he cares about his customer and his workforce and I'm the same. I know I rant and rave a lot, but I'm a softie at heart and I'd rather do something really well, make less on it and make sure the customer and the staff are happy. To that end I'm probably not the best businessman in the world because my heart is too big.

'I'm probably not the best businessman in the world because my heart is too big.'

As for some of the weird and wonderful things I do in the call centre – is it for a purpose? Is it going to make me more money? Maybe it will and maybe it won't. But if it makes for a productive, family environment then that's what matters to me. There was a moment at the 'Piss-up in a Brewery' when Hayley spontaneously started singing 'We Are Family' which really touched me because I've tried to create a family unity in my company. Yes families fall out, yes you're always going to have arguments, but fundamentally there's a strong bond between us which I find really moving. It all goes back to my saying, that 'the heart of the matter is a matter of the heart.' Ultimately we're just ordinary Swansea people trying to get through life, a bunch of morons who have been thrown together, ready to take on the world.

I take having fun very seriously and I like to lead with laughter. It's incredibly important to keep the atmosphere up in the call centre and silly challenges like the egg smashing contest mean that thanks to ten minutes of mucking about beforehand, by the time their shift starts everyone is buzzing. Energising the floor is important because if you've got a flat sales floor, the deals won't come in so fast. You need to feel the energy when you go through the door and sometimes it isn't there, so you have to create it. Like the Custard Pie Challenge, that competition started with Twe going: 'Who thinks I'm a bellend?'

'We all think you're a bellend, Twe.'

'Right, who wants to put a custard pie in my face?'

'We'd all like to put a custard pie in your face, Twe.'

'Excellent. You get ten deals today, you can put a custard pie in my face. You get eight deals you can put a custard pie in your team leader's face. If you don't make four sales, you'll get a custard pie in YOUR face!'

Everyone was up for it because they knew it was going to turn a potentially dull day into a fun day. Then you get all these HR types saying, 'Oh no that's illegal, you can't put pies in people's faces'. Did we have one person complain? No. It's a laugh, it's the banter, it's the beat. You've got to keep the beat going. If you go into the call centre you've got to feel that beat.

Another way to be different as a boss is to admit when you're wrong. It's no good being deluded thinking you're the best boss in the world and there's nothing new for you to learn. You're constantly

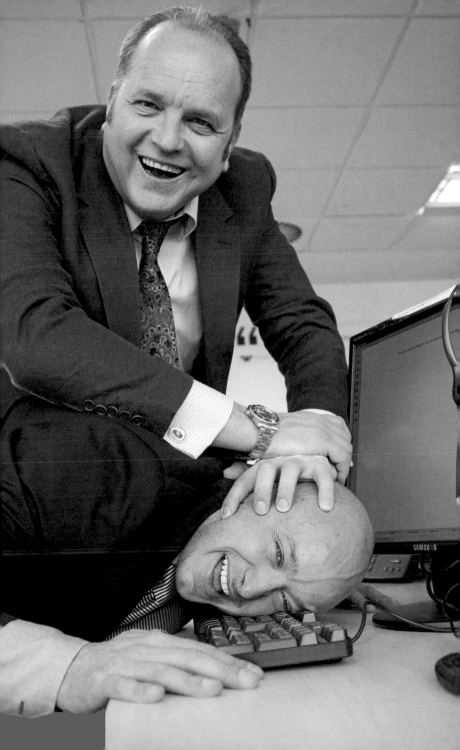

'I take having fun very seriously and I like to lead with laughter.'

learning, you're constantly improving. I've learnt along the way not to let accountants or the bank (those thieving bastards!) run your business. I keep telling my accountants, 'I run the business. The business is run by flair, ingenuity and hard work. Do not try and tell me how to run my business because that is not your job! I'll bat and bowl. You keep score.'

I have been known to bludgeon my way through situations and I'm learning that I can't be all guns blazing all the time. But sometimes you do need to take a situation by the balls and drive it, because if you don't no-one else is going to do it for you. Look at what Napoleon did as Emperor of France. Did he make mistakes? Of course he did, because he got way too big for his boots. And the lesson from that is a successful leader can't let their ego get out of control. If you ever see me getting too big for my boots just shoot me. You need to remember where you come from... and I'll never forget I'm just an arsehole from Swansea!

SOME WILL
SOME WON'T
SO WHAT?
NEXT!

CHAPTER

9

'I love to spread the love.'

Office relationships

There are those who believe that relationships in the workplace undermine professionalism, while others think they increase productivity and motivation. In my opinion, if two people that work for me find their way into a longterm relationship then the call centre can only become a happier place.

I love playing Cupid and I enjoy giving employees a helping hand into a steady loving relationship – Sir Alex Ferguson did the same. Did he want his boys to settle down? Of course he did. He didn't want them out partying every night, he wanted them settled. If you can get your employees into a stable relationship they work harder, they're more secure in themselves and they're more content in their lives. That's a fact. Whereas if they're out putting it about night after night it isn't good for business because their mind isn't on the job. Whether Chickenhead is getting a quick bonk is of no interest to me. Chickenhead's in love is he? Yeah, right. Don't look at your calendars, look at your watch. How long's that going to last?

Some companies ban relationships between employees which I think is a bit harsh. Barack and Michelle Obama met while working together at a Chicago law firm and they haven't done too badly, have they? But I'm aware that issues can arise if the relationship is with your direct manager. It's fine if two

people in similar positions start going out, where it can get messy is when the team leader sets about shagging everybody on his team. I really do not like that.

Take our resident South African Office Romeo, as I call him. He's a good motivator and a good worker, but when he was a team-leader I nearly sacked him when I heard he'd been bragging about shagging every girl on his team. I was like, 'A word from your sponsor... this is stopping RIGHT NOW!' and I gave him a good slap. It's about being professional; if you're in a more senior position that commands a bit of respect, don't let the power go to your head, but use it to look after those under you.

In my experience a loved-up happy workforce means more smiles and more productivity. It's good for morale because when you're in a happy relationship you love life that little bit more. If you're feeling down, if your boyfriend or girlfriend has just dumped you, I say to everyone, 'It's pointless you coming in because you're not going to sell anything mumbling away in miserable monotone – you're just going to bring the customers down with you!'

'Chickenhead's in love?
Don't look at your calendars,
look at your watch. How long's
that going to last?'

SWSWSWN!

Some will, some won't, so what – next! It's a sales
term I use a lot to remind the staff that you can't take
it personally every time someone hangs up on you or
slams a door in your face. Don't let those situations
get you down – you've got to move on immediately.
So adapt that sales thinking into your life outside of
work, because it's the same attitude that's needed when
it comes to your love-life. When Kayleigh in admin
was sobbing away that her life was ruined because
her relationship had ended, I told her: 'Your life is
not ruined. You went out with him for three bloody
months, your life is not ruined! Get over it. Move on.
Some will, some won't, so what – next!'

Gorgeous George

Nothing makes me happier than seeing my employees fall in love, but trying to find a date for George was one of the biggest challenges I've ever faced. The poor bastard hadn't had a bonk for six years and he was the only one on the speed-dating night who didn't get a date. We put posters up around the office with George's head on Brad Pitt's body in a bid to kickstart things, I wanted to try and lighten the situation for him because he was in despair. He was really starting to get down about it. But he still couldn't get a girl. After the series went out the local radio station and the local press took it upon themselves to get George a date. They had about six people lined up, but every one of them backed out at the last minute, even though he'd been given a make-over and came out looking like a Greek god. However, I can now exclusively reveal that George did get laid – by someone from Northampton, no less. It was a tough slog, but we got him there in the end, to the rapturous applause of the call centre!

Nev Wilshire

CHAPTER

10

'The feather or the mallet.'

Maintaining discipline

The happy-clappy environment we try to create can lead to employees taking the piss. Or even shitting in a bin. So there are days when you have to sit people down and remind them where to draw the line. Yes, this is a fun place to work, but you need to set out the parameters, the rules and regulations for your business that everyone understands and abides by. As a boss I try to lead by example and inspire my employees to maintain a suitable reputation for the business. I try my best to encourage and nurture them, but if they cross the line they're going to get a slap. I call this technique the feather or the mallet – you start off with a feather, subtly tickling people into doing what you want. But if that doesn't work you've got to come down hard on them and hit them over the head with the mallet in order to make them do what you want. Beware, if you're not going to get there with a tickle, I'm going to flippin' well clobber you – metaphorically speaking of course!

'If you're not going to get there with a tickle, I'm going to flippin' well clobber you!'

How to handle bad behaviour

Turn the tables...

Chickenhead was a disruptive influence so we taught him a lesson by making him responsible for the company football team. As a result he finally realised how difficult it is trying to organise arseholes like him!

Conflict spreads...

...so nip it in the bud. If someone's disruptive you've got to look at the bigger picture. You can try to be a peacemaker but if that doesn't work (even if they're your biggest seller) you need to move them on.

Separate disruptive influences...

Griff and Chickenhead had to be split up because they were behaving like naughty schoolboys. Sometimes I do feel like a headmaster – if only I could give them six of the best!

Final warning

You can change almost anything about a person except for the attitude. The heart of the matter is a matter of the heart and if your heart isn't in it – see ya! If someone has an attitude problem then I don't want them on my team because whatever you asked them to do the outcome would be disappointing. If you asked someone with a bad attitude to make you a cup of tea, I can guarantee it'd be a shit cup of tea. So if new recruits aren't interested on their first day of training then they really aren't going to be interested a couple of weeks down the line, so there's the door, bugger off. There's more to life than being unhappy in a job. If you wake up and think, 'Oh bugger, I've got to be at work with that Nev nob-head', go and do something else. Jack it in!

'The heart of the matter is a matter of the heart and if your heart isn't in it – see ya!'

It's a sackable offence!

1. Refusing to sing.
2. Shitting in a bin.
3. Being rude to customers or hanging up on them.
4. Getting 'over amorous' with a maintenance man in the office.
5. Throwing grapes at each other.
6. Shagging at an office party.
   (NB. These all actually happened)

Dress code

Some of the younger girls will try and outdo each other in order to attract a guy's attention. The skirts will suddenly go very short so I have to say, 'Excuse me you're not coming in here like that. Go home and change!' And it's not just the girls. I've seen boys who are so busy trying to look perfect they don't give a monkey's about doing their job, so their sales are crap. So I don't mind all the preening that goes on if it keeps them entertained at their desks, but if it starts to affect their sales, that's when I get out my mallet.

First appearances matter and in my opinion if you dress well you feel better. If you wear a smart suit and a tie your posture, your attitude and your whole demeanour changes. It's a psychological thing. You don't just look more professional, you feel it. I know people who work from home who still put on a suit everyday just to get that mindset right. In business you dress for success. Slobby dress leads to slobby attitude. Fact.

The kick up the arse

The kick up the arse is a punishment that demonstrates who's in charge, in case staff members get confused about the pecking order. For example, one time this lad kept turning up late blaming it on the buses. 'Word from your sponsor son, don't give me this shit. Do you think I haven't heard this hundreds of times before? Right, you've got two choices; I could send you down to HR and they can give you a disciplinary warning or... I can just kick you up the arse? What do you want?' More often than not they take the kick up the arse. So I get them to bend over, I whack them where the sun don't shine, then I ask them for the special words which are 'Thank you Nev' and tell them to piss off and sort themselves out. Because if this happens again they're going straight to HR.

CASE STUDY

To: nevtheboss@savebritainmoney.co.uk
From: becca_HR@savebritainmoney.co.uk

Subject: **Kicking staff**

REMOVE ANY MENTION OF THIS FROM THE
BOOK. Have you actually gone mad! What next?
Are you going to tell them about the time you
overdosed on sherbet lemons and ran dancing
through the office singing 'Sex On Fire'? (Obviously
do NOT include that either.)
Please get back to me ASAP.

Becca

CHAPTER

11

'Smile as you dial.'

The perfect telesale

I try to drill into my team that everyone is in sales to some extent – you wouldn't have a boyfriend or a girlfriend if you hadn't had to sell yourself to somebody, show off your best attributes and pretend to be nice. Fundamentally these skills are within all of us – some take to it like a duck to water, others need months to hit their stride.

Some people say sales is an art – I say it's a science. Yes, you need to be creative and have a flair for it, but if you don't work hard it's not going to happen. You've got to bust a gut because the more you put into it, the more you're going to get out of it. The more doors you knock, the more people are going to say yes. And all the time you need to be smiling because no-one's going to buy from a miserable-looking bastard.

It's the same on the phones; if you smile before you dial your voice changes, your pitch changes and your enthusiasm is palpable. A smile is infectious even over the phone. When you are talking to a potential customer they can sense whether you're smiling or not, because they aren't going to listen to you if you sound bored. Yes, you may be having a shitty day, but there's no reason for the person on the other end of the line to be aware of that. When you're smiling it's hard to sound like you're in a bad mood – try it!

When I worked door-to-door my sales manager handed me one of the best pieces of advice I've ever been given: don't be too cool for school; ask open questions and before you knock think of something that really makes you laugh so you can greet the customer with a genuine smile. Right, my brother

We have over a 90% success rate !!!

WE CLAIM U GAIN

Keith was a fit, good-looking, 6' 8", 24 year-old strapping lad... and then he started losing his hair! He stuck with it for four years before shaving it off. That image is still guaranteed to make me laugh and it worked each time I rapped on a new door. I'd picture Keith, there's the stupid smiley grin and then 'Knock knock, sorry to bother you...' and on you go with the sales pitch. It's not a forced Tony Blair smile with those dead eyes – it's a bright-eyed genuine smile and I'll tell you what, it works every bloody time!

How to smile

A step-by-step guide for miserable bastards...

Step 1
Think happy thoughts... e.g. Keith losing his hair.

Step 2
Smile with your eyes... everybody loves a twinkle.

3

4

Step 3

The key is smiling wide... show the top row of your teeth.

Step 4

Hold it for as long as you can... without looking like a constipated fart!

A good salesperson will always...

See the glass half full

Spot the opportunity, the market and the need. For example, a shoe salesman goes to a far-flung island. He's greeted by the natives but stops dead in his tracks at what he sees. 'Oh no – they don't wear shoes!' So he gets back on the boat and sails home. 'Boss...' he sighs, 'that was a bloody waste of time.' A few weeks later another salesman heads out, but he starts rubbing his hands with glee at what he sees. 'Yes!' he cries. 'None of them have shoes – I'm gonna sell shit-loads!' Salesman no. 2 has the right idea, it's about looking at your product with a glass half full perspective as opposed to a glass half empty. Am I a glass half full or half empty kind of person? My answer to that is GET ME A BIGGER GLASS!

'Am I a glass half full or half empty kind of person? My answer to that is GET ME A BIGGER GLASS!'

Sell the benefits

In my company we deal in cavity wall insulation which frankly is not the most interesting product in the world. So we offer it to the customer by selling the BENEFITS. We're selling comfort (because you'll be warmer in winter and cooler in summer), we're selling a reduction in noise pollution, we're selling huge savings on your energy bills. The customer doesn't give a crap about the actual white stuff that goes into the wall because they're never going to see it. So you always sell the benefits, because saving time and money (and the ability to allow your customer to have more of them) are the greatest benefits anyone can sell.

Cope with rejection

Don't take abuse personally. Maybe that person's dog has just died, maybe they've just had a bereavement or an argument with the wife. Try and humanise the person you're calling – we all have bad days when we don't want to chat to a stranger on the phone. It's not your fault, so remember: SWSWSWN! Some will, some won't, so what – next! Before the next dial, dust yourself down, think of something that will make you smile (Keith losing his hair) and put it behind you. I will not tolerate my employees slamming the phone down on anyone – regardless of what's happened – you put the phone down politely.

Can you feel it?

'Feel Felt Found' is a proven technique when handling objections to a sale.

Feel...

'I understand how you FEEL about that Mrs Jones...' (This indicates you're listening and can empathise with the customer.)

Felt...

'My sister FELT the same...' ('Safety in numbers' demonstrates to the customer they're not alone in their objection.)

Found...

'She was dubious at first but what she FOUND was it would save her more than £200 a month.' (Revealing that others with the same objection found that not only was everything all right – it was better than ever!)

Once you've tried it a few times I can guarantee this will become an integral part of your sales patter. At first you may feel a bit self-conscious about it, many of our new recruits felt the same, but when they tried it on the phones they found it worked a treat and bagged them lots of lovely sales!

My guide to the perfect telesale...

Get to the point...

It's all very well being chatty and engaging the customer, but people don't want to listen to you waffling all day. We give our employees a script for reference but tell them not to use it or else they will bore people to death. Your initial goal is to get through the first five seconds without anyone putting the phone down on you. Remember you can talk yourself out of a sale by rabbiting on too much.

Know your product...

I've read training material that says attitude is more important than knowledge. I'd say that's bollocks. Knowledge is vital. You can't sell your product if you don't know your product. On top of that you need to know your whole market inside and out. NO means the customer does not KNOW enough. If you've got something they could benefit from and they don't want it, then you haven't explained the benefits to them properly.

Consider your audience...

Connect with each person on a human level and
adapt your patter to suit them. Give everything
a positive spin, but don't be over familiar. People
appreciate flattery, they don't like bullshit. Sales is
a contact sport and if you don't connect with the
customer you aren't going to sell anything. Listening
is important too, take the conversation where you
want it to go by moving the goalposts towards
making that sale.

Be Welsh...

If your voice sounds confident and professional you will be taken seriously. An assured voice puts people at ease and if the customer believes you can deliver your promises then you're going to make the sale. In my mind you can't beat a Welsh accent because the tone is both comforting and reassuring. If you're Welsh you already have a head-start on the Cockneys and the Scousers – two accents that always make me feel I'm about to be conned!

Remember the ABC of sales...

Always Be Closing. Once you have sold the benefits you've got to ask for the order. If you see a beautiful blonde by the bar and you don't ask her out... guess what? She's not gonna go out with you! If you don't ask for the sale you aren't going to get it. At the end of my spiel I always use the phrase, 'So, are you happy with that?' It's a nice friendly way of saying 'Do you want to buy it?' Minimise opportunities for them to say no. Don't say 'Are you happy with that or not?' That 'or not' is the last thing they hear and immediately plants a seed of doubt in their mind.

'If you're Welsh you already have a head-start on Cockneys and Scousers – two accents that always make me feel I'm about to be conned!'

'I've been rich and I've been poor –
rich is much better.'

Tough times

A businessman in trouble is a lonely place to be.
People you thought were your friends disappear,
you're on your own and you carry the burden of
responsibility for an awful lot of people. That's a lot
of pressure and let's not bullshit, when my business
went bust I was on my arse. It was a horrible time
and I wouldn't wish it on anybody; it contributed to
my divorce and affected lots of people's lives. In that
situation what you have to remember is that, yes, they
can take your business away from you, but they can't
foreclose on your life. And while I was too dispirited to
realise it at the time, there is value in making mistakes
because ultimately it makes you a better businessman.

Otherwise you plough on thinking you're invincible, thinking you're doing everything fantastically well when you're not. If you learn from defeat you haven't really lost. The fact is that everybody in business will have highs and lows during their career, and if you haven't yet... you're going to!

There's a quote from our great leader Winston Churchill which has always resonated with me: 'Success is not final, failure is not fatal. It is the courage to continue that counts.' When the chips are down you've got to fight even harder, you've got to focus your mind without panicking and you've got to battle on through. The British bulldog spirit and all that. When you're down in the depths the only way is up, and like another of my heroes John Wayne would've done, you have to get back on the horse and discover new frontiers, cowboy! You can't sit on your arse waiting for things to come to you, you've got to roll up your sleeves, get out there, get stuck in and make things happen.

There's always plenty of business out there, you just have to dedicate yourself to the cause and keep battling on in order to get it. Because if you take your finger off the pulse for one minute, someone else will take the initiative. Someone else more hungry and determined will steal those potential clients off you. Ultimately there's no reason for a good salesman to be out of business – a good salesman will go and sell himself to somebody else!

Taking the Mickey

Just before I went bust, I'd paid the deposit on a holiday to Disneyworld, which is my favourite place on the planet. My mum and dad paid the balance, as we needed a family holiday, and six months later we headed out to Orlando. But I was feeling very sorry for myself. I tried to put on a brave face and pretend I was fine, but I wasn't. On the spur of the moment I went to see *The Walt Disney Story* and it ended up being a lightbulb moment for me. It turned out that he'd gone bust not once, but twice! But Walt's brother Roy and his parents had such faith in Walt that they invested everything they had in his vision. And such was his own belief in his product that each time he'd picked himself up and tried again, not only in a recession like me but in the middle of the depression! That man's strength of character was an inspiration and gave me the kick up the backside I needed to pull myself together. I'd gone bust once, I was hurting, but I was being a wuss. Walt Disney said, 'Unless you have tasted failure you will not handle success', and having experienced both I can only agree with him.

Nev Wilshire

CHAPTER

13

'The art of communication is the language of leadership.'

Communications

Effective communication is a no-brainer because when those channels break down you're left with demotivated employees, poor productivity and (even scarier) a grumpy boss! Many new businesses fail not because their idea was bad but because nobody knew how good their idea was. You have to communicate it and that can be internal as well – you need to explain to your team why you do things in a certain way. If you don't properly communicate the vision internally, your staff aren't going to be able to communicate it to the customer properly either. Luckily I love the sound of my own voice so I'm forever communicating whether anyone is listening or not. Here are my top tips for improving your gob-shite skills...

Give good feedback...

No employee wants to feel like they exist in a vacuum. Praise the positives. Your staff need to know they're valued and their efforts are recognised.

Be visible...

Some bosses are distant figures and employees struggle to identify them. Obviously there's no danger of that while I'm around – you can hear me in the building before I've even parked up outside.

Revive the art of conversation...

I like to get to know each and every staff member and find out what aspirations they may have. They can also give you feedback as to what's working and what isn't.

Say it face to face...

We now have more ways than ever to communicate, but I'd rather tell you something to your face. I have never done a deal on email. Make eye contact instead.

Spread the credit...

Inspiring leaders don't take all the glory for themselves. Redirect praise towards the others on your team.

Give accolades...

Particularly if someone has gone above and beyond the call of duty. A promotion or bonus will make them feel 10 feet tall and you'll reap the benefits.

Be approachable...

My door is always open if anyone needs me. It's the
sign of an inspirational boss when your employees turn
to you for guidance.

'I love the sound of
my own voice so I'm
forever communicating.'

The Shit Sandwich

How do you engage with 20-somethings and bollock them at the same time? Easy, have a regular staff meeting and call it 'The Shit Sandwich'. This management technique works on the basis that younger people open up to negative feedback far more if you start off by complimenting them (the first slice of bread), then give them the bollocking (the shit) and finally finish on another positive (slice of bread no. 2). If you were to go straight in with shit you'd have lost them from the start. See right...

Fork filching

Around 100 forks were disappearing from the kitchen every month – all I could think was, 'Why are they stealing my forks? Stop stealing my flippin' forks!' So I needed to address this blatant theft between two bits of good news:

The first slice of bread: 'Well done everyone, last week's sales were an all-time record. Give yourselves a round of applause!'

Now the shit: 'You've gone through a hundred forks this month. Stop stealing my bloody forks or I'm going to search your bags on a daily basis. Got it?'

The second slice of bread: 'By the way, as a reward for the record sales we've got a bouncy castle coming to the car-park this afternoon. Who wants a bounce with Nev?!'

So it's praise and positives on either side with some serious bollocking in the middle. You've got to leave them on a high, as they are going back to the phones to sell!

CASE STUDY

To: nevtheboss@savebritainmoney.co.uk
From: becca_HR@savebritainmoney.co.uk

Subject: **Foul language**

Nev

Do you have to use the nasty s-word here? Could we perhaps change it to 'silly-sausage' sandwich instead?

Becca

14

'Choose a job you love and you'll never have to work a day in your life.'

Work–life balance

In this country we like to compartmentalise things, we like to separate everything out – work-time, family-time, fun-time – whereas many other cultures don't do that. They just think about life as a whole and everything is embodied within that. Work and life is all interlinked for me too – I don't think about separating them out because I just have a life and my work is a major part of that.

You could say I'm a workaholic. Whether that's a good thing or not I do not know, but to be able to love

your work and enjoy what you do is such a wonderful
thing and makes you want to go the extra mile. I've
heard it said that if you're still in the office at 8pm then
you're doing something wrong: you aren't on top of
your job, you aren't delegating properly. I disagree. I
could cut people short and not bother getting to know
my staff. I could stop bothering to train the new starter
groups, I could cut my work time down so I get out
at 5 o'clock on the dot and I could work three days a
week if I chose. Or I can continue the way I'm doing
it by getting to know these people, trying to enhance
their lives and by doing so enhancing my business at
the same time.

I'd come across as very selfish if I became obsessed
with maintaining a work–life balance and thought,
'F*ck this, I'm going to swan around and leave these
bastards to do all the hard work.' That's not what
it's all about for me because I love my work and I'm
passionate about it. How much time you spend in the
workplace is an individual thing and everyone has to
find a framework that works for them. My life is in
Swansea running my business. Sod the work and life
balance, to me it's all one and the same.

'Sod the work and life
balance, to me it's all
one and the same.'

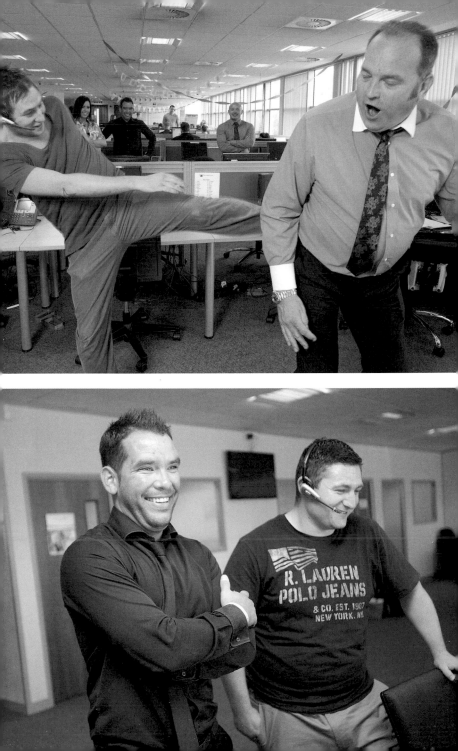

Choose life!

Despite my rant above, you do need to look after your own health and wellbeing while in the workplace. Nobody wants to find their boss dead at his desk...

Don't get bogged down in detail...
A good boss needs to know when to step back. Keep your finger on the pulse, but focus on the bigger picture.

Delegate...
Surround yourself with good people and the rest is easy. It empowers your employees and means they'll take pride in their work.

Take regular breaks...
You're more productive and efficient if you take breaks during the working day. Get Hayley to make you a cup of T-coffee and it will help you de-stress!

Address the adrenalin...

You can only survive on adrenalin for short bursts. Avoid running on empty and keep energised with regular snacks and exercise.

Learn to say no...

I struggled to say no for a while, but you've got to learn that you can't do everything yourself. Speak up when the work demands become too much.

Have clear goals...

Know where you're heading and how to get there. If you're dithering or unsure you will only make extra work for yourself in the long run.

Take a holiday...

Everybody needs time off and on your return you'll be raring to go with your drive reinvigorated. Even the sight of Chickenhead will put a smile on your face!

CHAPTER

15

'The best way to predict the future is to create it.'

Follow your dreams

I could never have envisioned that our business would grow to this size, it's beyond my wildest dreams of a few years ago and the possibilities for the future are massive. The truth is you don't always have a grand plan, but you do need to know the direction you're going in. It's like you're building a house, brick by brick, floor by floor. If you want it to get bigger it is up to you to make it happen, because it's not going to build itself. If you're not thinking about the vision you're not going to get anywhere. The best way to predict the future is to create it and I'm forever declaring the vision to my team. You're always going to be subject to circumstances, but when obstacles arise you change your direction to reach your goal, you do not change your original decision to get there. A message for life as well as business.

You have to believe in your business with all your heart and what defines a true entrepreneur is to go beyond worrying about the risks and what could go wrong, and just do it. Don't let being scared stop you from pursuing something you really want to do. You have to become fearless. You have to take risks. But calculated risks not foolish risks; although there have been a few times I have put my arse in a sling and gone for it. It isn't all method, it may not work out, you may have the best ideas in the world and sometimes it still won't succeed. But unless you go for it, how will you ever know?

My dream from an early age was to be a businessman – I always recognised that was where I was heading. So think about what YOU are meant to be. If you were meant to be a footballer, train hard, practice and be a footballer. Even if you get doors shut in your face, keep knocking. Find your level and grow from there. Maybe you're a David Beckham or a Ryan Giggs, but most of us aren't that good so let's start playing for Stockport instead. Start small and don't aim to be Microsoft overnight – occasionally that happens but it's very rare.

If you want to grow your business you've got to put every ounce of your being into it. You need to have the

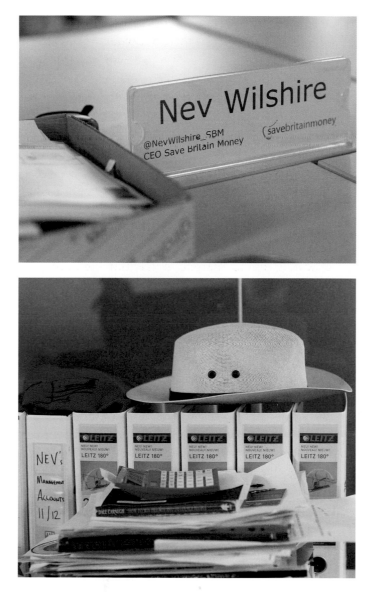

hunger to win and I can't overstate enough the need
for hard work. Here are my final words of advice – use
your God-given gifts, treat others as you'd like to be
treated and WORK HARD. Things aren't going to
fall into your lap. Success is directly proportionate to
the effort you put in. If kids come into the call centre
and think in six months time they'll be living the
dream then they're going to get a shock. Because life
is a marathon not a sprint. Sometimes you've got to
sprint as part of the marathon, still most of the time
it's a slog. But if you're inclined to work for it, with a
smile on your face and a song in your heart – then that
dream could become a reality!

'When obstacles arise you change your direction to reach your goal, you do not change your original decision to get there.'

This book is published to accompany the television series entitled *The Call Centre*, first broadcast on BBC Three in June 2013.

Executive Producers: Samantha Anstiss, Aysha Rafaele and Tim Green
Produced by: Jon Connerty
Directed by: Xavier Alford, Jacci Parry, Oliver Cheetham and Joe Ward

1 3 5 7 9 10 8 6 4 2

Published in 2013 by BBC Books, an imprint of Ebury Publishing.
A Random House Group Company.

The Random House Group Limited Reg. No. 954009

Addresses for companies within the Random House Group can be found at www.randomhouse.co.uk

A CIP catalogue record for this book is available from the British Library.

ISBN: 9781849907408

The Random House Group Limited supports The Forest Stewardship Council (FSC®), the leading international forest certification organisation. Our books carrying the FSC label are printed on FSC® certified paper. FSC is the only forest certification scheme endorsed by the leading environmental organisations, including Greenpeace. Our paper procurement policy can be found at www.randomhouse.co.uk/environment

Commissioning editor: Lorna Russell
Project editor: Kate Fox
Design and typesetting: Estuary English

Printed and bound by Firmengruppe APPL, aprinta druck, Wemding, Germany

To buy books by your favourite authors and register for offers visit www.randomhouse.co.uk